ANCHOR BOOKS

AND THE NIGHTS DRAW IN

Edited by

Rachael Radford

First published in Great Britain in 2003 by
ANCHOR BOOKS
Remus House,
Coltsfoot Drive,
Peterborough, PE2 9JX
Telephone (01733) 898102

All Rights Reserved

Copyright Contributors 2003

HB ISBN 1 84418 092 1
SB ISBN 1 84418 093 X

FOREWORD

And The Nights Draw In is a collection of uplifting and inspiring poems from many of today's new and established authors. Together they unite to reflect on the beauty around them, during the magical autumn and winter months.

Each of the poets freely share these inspirations in life by using their creative talent to mould and express a picture of their views to others.

With over 100 poems inside, this book is a companion for life, to be read time and time again.

Rachael Radford
Editor

CONTENTS

Autumn Is Here	E Woodham	1
Prelude	Barbara Robson	2
A New Autumn	Zoe French	3
Watch In Wonder	Deanna L Dixon	4
Trees In Late Autumn	E Balmain	5
Autumn	N Ferguson	6
Grandfather Christmas	Denis Shiels	7
Glamorous Autumn	Milly Hatcher	8
Turning Cold	S Mitchell	9
Autumn Air	B Page	10
Autumnal Thoughts	John Paulley	11
Autumn Treasures	Gloria Beeston	12
The Rich Autumnal Fall	Jill Darroch	13
. . . And So Autumn	Rob Purcell	14
Autumn	Rozetta Pate	15
Autumn	Jackie Davies	16
Autumn	David Sheasby	17
The Bramble Patch Mysteries	Derek Harvey	18
Stop, Look And Listen	Rachel Mary Mills	19
Observing Autumn	Thora Carpenter	20
Autumn	Sheila Storr	21
Winter's On Its Way	Christine Nolan	22
Autumn Dusk	Sandra L Hopwood	23
Death In Autumn	Sid 'de' Knees	24
Leaf Fall	Kathleen M Hatton	25
Autumn Treats	Lois M Pester	26
Autumn Remembers	Meryl	27
September Song	Joan M Jones	28
The Autumnal Changes 2002	Stella Bush-Payne	29
Autumn Thoughts	J M Gardener	30
Something Different About Autumn	Margie Fox	31
Summer's Death	V M McKinley	32
That Autumn	Ray Smith	33
Scenes Of Autumn	Michelle Luetchford	34
Autumn Leaves	Doris Livesey	35

As Autumn Fades	Irene Grahame	36
November	P Rock	38
The Fairy's Story	Vivienne Roberts	39
Ducks Of Cuerden Park	Robert Allen	40
Extra Special	Lorna Lea	41
Autumn	Sylvia Shafto	42
The Other View Of Autumn	R Hannam	43
Autumn Music	Clive Anderson	44
The Gift Of Autumn	Ruth Shallard	45
Observing Autumn	F R Smith	46
Autumn Magic	Helen T Westley	47
November Lament	Savile Sykes	48
Summer To Fall	Julie Tucker	49
The Colour Of Autumn	Rosalind Jennings	50
Observing Autumn	Joanna Young	51
Autumn	Rosalind I Caygill	52
Autumn Leaves	Jean Lloyd-Williams	53
Pictured Rain	T McFarlane	54
Santa Claus	Annette Murphy	55
Outlook Unsettled	Dennis Marshall	56
Seasonal Affected Disorder	R Bowhill	57
Autumn	Catherine Armstrong	58
Autumn	Pamela Carder	59
Autumn	June Davies	60
Autumn Slumbers	Kaz	61
Autumn Walk	White Knight	62
Late Autumn	Tony Gyimes	63
Set Fare For Autumn	Vera Morrill	64
The Autumn Of Life	Jackie Barker-Smith	66
November Morning	Christopher S Mills	67
Autumn	Ellen Thompson	68
Mists Of Autumn	J Millington	69
A Child's Autumn	Valerie Catterall	70
Observing Autumn	Monica Wood	71
Scenes Of Autumn	Elizabeth Amy Johns	72
Autumn	Jillian Mounter	73
Ode To Rain	Elizabeth Morton	74
Autumn Rain	Robert Simpson	75

Title	Author	Page
Autumn	V Hankins	76
Seedlings	Joseph McGarraghy	77
Mellow Season	Iris E Weller	78
Autumn In The Purbecks	A M Craven	79
Prelude To Winter	Michael Close	80
Seascape	Hazel Sheppard	81
Autumn Days	Doris Lilian Critchley	82
Wild, Wild Winds	Lorna June Burdon	83
Autumn Shades	Ann Linney	84
Autumn	Sylvia Partridge	85
Ode To Autumn	Joan McLoughlin	86
Autumn	Jack Scrafton	87
Autumn Colours	Christine Cyster	88
Autumn	R W Cummings	89
Autumn	Monica D Buxton	90
Autumn Reflections	Rosalia Campbell Orr	91
Swallows Gather	Pam Hatcher	92
The Autumn Boy	Margo Mallett	93
Wintertime	Margaret Andrews Sherrington	94
Bramble Jelly!	Roy A Millar	95
Autumnal Stroll	George S Johnstone	96
Odium To Winter	Ron Hails	98
As Summer Turns To Autumn	Angela Moore	100
Conker Time	David A Garside	101
Overcast	Dale Mullock	102
October Rain	A P Starling	103
A Rainy Day	Jean P McGovern	104
Written In The Rain	B Clark	105
Pool Of Tears	Ray Smith	106
The Storm	A Howells	107

AUTUMN IS HERE

Once again the nights draw in,
The colder days are going to win,
The leaves are turning red and brown,
The trees look like a golden crown,
The swallows all have flown away
And farmers gathered in their hay,
Small animals will hibernate,
The robin stays, perched on the gate,
The mower we can put away.
No grass to cut until a spring day.
The leaves want moving with a rake
And then a bonfire we can make.
It's time to get out the preserving pan,
To make our chutneys, pickles and jam.
The wind is howling while I'm in bed,
I'm glad my prayers have all been said,
Autumn is here, then it's winter and spring,
Look at the joys when the birds start to sing,
Let's sit by the fire and read a nice book
And think of the lovely hot meals we can cook,
Let's tuck up in bed, is that fireworks I hear?
I'll dream, but I can't wait till the snowdrops are here!

E Woodham

PRELUDE

September the prelude to autumn
Like young true love all aglow
With warm arms she gently enfolds you
Have you not found it so?

The air is alive with piquancy
Melded smells and colours combined
Wood fire smoke and chrysanthemums
Red berries hips and rowan, vibrancy unconfined

Mellow autumn I love you
Gold leaf leaves crunch under my feet
Indigo sky when darkness falls
A shock of stars and the day is complete.

Barbara Robson

A NEW AUTUMN

Every year a new autumn will arrive.
Through the red and golden leaves kids can dive.
The conkers on the trees are ready to drop.
Blackberries on the briers will not stop.
People picking them for jams and pies.
Apples on the trees branches reaching for the skies.
Soon the apple pickers will divest the trees.
Before the fruit could fall in a stiff breeze.
Squirrels hiding nuts and acorns hoping to find them
                                            in the ice and snow.
If they don't find them then next year they will grow.
Rabbits looking for the last of the greens.
Foxes looking for the rabbits as yet unseen.
The farmer with his tractor turning the soil potatoes to reveal.
People picking the potatoes up and putting them in sacks to await a seal.
The wheat in sheaves and bails with plastic fitted over them
                                            to keep out the rain.
Smoke drifting from the bonfires over hill and plain.
Flowers giving off their last in the evening chill.
Before they wither and die except those inside on a window sill.
The spider's web made pretty by glistening drops of the morning dew.
All the berries on bushes and trees especially the yew.
The birds singing their farewell song.
Winter is coming and it won't be long.

Zoe French

WATCH IN WONDER

I stare into my coffee cup,
trying hard to wake up.
I watch the cold October morn,
spread its light across my lawn.
I listen as birds begin to speak,
trilling through their tiny beaks.
Look as blue, colours the sky,
and the sun bids the moon goodbye.
Smell the sweet morning air,
feel the dampness that lingers there.
No longer staring in my coffee cup,
I watch with wonder, as the world wakes up.

Deanna L Dixon

TREES IN LATE AUTUMN

Archway of boughs, bare arms entwined,
Reaching to heaven in muted praise,
Crowned with nests, deserted now,
Entering their winter phase.
What fantasy of sculptured forms!
Their stark, white boles displaying,
So different now from earlier times
When once we went a-maying.
Each mossy growth green 'gainst the bark,
Each flaky crevice sharp revealed,
What's that extruding from the earth?
A naked root, snake like, congealed.
Yet here some faint remains of leaves
Of brown and red, and golden hues
Shows that their glory is not dead,
Waits in the wings till spring gives cues.

E Balmain

AUTUMN

Summer's work as last is ending
Nature triumphs once again
Orchard trees with fruits are bending
Fields are rich with golden grain

Harvest then these bounteous presents
Gather them with gratitude
Thankfulness must be the essence
Flavouring the harvest food

Beauty too remains with autumn
Nature surely loves the land
Such scenes she paints are ne'er forgotten
Evidence of her loving hand

But sadness too is mingled here,
When those joyous days have died
Cold days of winds and storms appear
For winter will not be denied.

But faith will always see us through it
Hope sustain our hearts and then
Joy is not lost, spring will renew it
For soon it will return again.

N Ferguson

GRANDFATHER CHRISTMAS

Louisa put her arms around my neck,
Showing not a sign of fear,
Mummy said, 'Kiss him,' she gave me a peck,
You see, it's that time of the year.

Time to draw children away from their tellies,
With promise of gifts from the sack,
To meet the old man in red coat and wellies
Beard and snow right down his back.

The long coat is hot and the hood is wet
And the wellies are terribly tight,
But, wearing a grin and ignoring the sweat,
It's the beginning of Christmas tonight!

It's the time when mums give their tinies a warning
They've got to be good girls and boys,
Or there'll be nothing there when they look in the morning
So, sleep now - no peeping - no noise . . .

Some babies draw away from a fierce Santa Claus
And cling to Mum with piercing cries,
Some are hesitant, and pause,
With doubting, but expectant eyes.

For many years I've donned the guise,
And played my willed parts,
To see their pleasure is my prize,
And to bring delight to happy hearts . . .

Denis Shiels

GLAMOROUS AUTUMN

The colours of the autumn makes my heart sing,
It brings out the beauty of everything.
Rosy - red apples and blackberries too,
A part of all God's gifts for you.

Bright yellow dandelions and purple heather,
Herald a mixture of autumn weather.
An Indian summer with sunshine bright -
Hot in the day, but cool at night.

Mist, slowly rising, uncovers the sight
Of little white mushrooms, that popped up overnight.
Strong winds blow the leaves off the trees,
To make red and gold carpets, before the big freeze.

Spiders in the bath, and in my hair
Spin their gossamer webs everywhere.
And the chime of bells on an autumn day
Sounds crisp and clear, but far away.

Then there's the smell on Bonfire night -
The fireworks make a wonderful sight.
Baked potatoes, wrapped in foil,
So the ashes will not spoil.

The long shadows of autumn
Mean winter is near -
But the joy of the autumn
Will be with us next year.

Milly Hatcher

TURNING COLD

Summer sun has faded,
The tourists gone away,
The cold of autumn creeping in,
To start another day.

The leaves are falling from the trees
They gently flutter down,
To form a big damp blanket,
Of deepest golden brown.

The plants and flowers dying,
The seeds hide far below,
Waiting for the warmer times,
When they can start to grow.

People huddled up in coats,
They hurry on their way,
Not wanting to be caught outside,
By a chilly autumn day.

Conkers, pine cones, bits of wood
Crackle as you walk,
You hear then as you walk along,
Too cold to even talk.

At home you have a toddy,
Honey and some rum,
Knowing that when autumn's gone,
There's even worse to come.

S Mitchell

Autumn Air

Autumn is a time of loss
When Nature sheds her gown
When in all the greenery she was dressed
Is now red, gold and brown.

The streets and parks now underfoot
Are filled with dying embers
From growth each tree and bush gave birth
From April to September.

The sun is low, in pale blue skies
Now Nature goes to rest
Preparing for those winter days
Now holly is at its best.

The morning dews are heavier now
There's dampness in the air
Nature continues to disrobe
Till everywhere is bare.

Birds that came to visit us
Are off to sunnier climes
But they'll be back again next year
When there's visible signs.

B Page

AUTUMNAL THOUGHTS

There is a nip in autumn air,
The cows in pastures stand and stare;
The leaves all turning shades of brown,
The log fires burning in The Crown.

The hedgerows lose their thickset look,
At home the family turn to books;
The squirrel hoards a load of nuts,
The crops are stored in frost-proof huts.

Some gentle frosts give rise to fear,
The animals know the time of year;
Their coats just thicken as cold winds blow,
The birds all gather before the snow.

The winter crops all sown in ground,
The farmers struggle with the pound;
The tortoise moves more slow each day,
The power of sunshine fades away.

Soon the leaves all gone from trees,
Soon the great big winter freeze;
Soon the heating turned up high,
Soon the snow will fall from sky.

Some things in autumn bring some joy,
The children play indoors with toys;
The colours, splendour, of the leaves,
Just cheer us up to face the freeze.

John Paulley

AUTUMN TREASURES

The delightful colours of autumn
So wonderful to behold -
So many different tones and shades
Of green and red and gold.

The trees take on different silhouettes
As the season changes;
And nature with its routine
The landscape re-arranges.

Animals start to change their coats,
Which makes sure that they stay warm,
So when the winter weather comes
They're not dejected or forlorn.

For autumn has its own charm
And its own mystique
And many interesting sights
If we care to peek.

Gloria Beeston

THE RICH AUTUMNAL FALL

When Nature paints her seasons,
Her pallet holds the key -
With abundant hues, from which to choose,
Which season can I see?
On the canvas set before me;
Is a masterpiece, so bold:
Suffused with crimsons, nutmeg browns -
Burnt amber, ochre, gold!
Warmth exudes, yet as I view,
The chill autumnal air,
Swirls and curls about my head -
Running fingers through my hair.
As I amble through this canvass,
Crisp crackles, where I tread:
Give warning to the squirrel,
As he scrambles overhead.
Evening shadows dance around -
As night descends, and soon,
A golden glow invades the sky,
Then I spy a harvest moon!
If I could own one masterpiece,
To hang upon my wall:
I'd chose the one entitled,
'The rich autumnal fall'.

Jill Darroch

... AND SO AUTUMN

... and so autumn has arrived
and the trees are again deprived
of the leaves that they have known
since springtime they have grown.

Leaves that were once green
now litter the scene
falling to the ground
a million shades of brown.

Onwards the air grows colder
and in the eye of the beholder
the trees are laid bare
as is custom every year.

Before long the greenery will return
when once again spring gets its turn
trees will once again flourish
on streets, in fields and in the forest.

Rob Purcell

Autumn

The lovely days of summer are coming to an end
the leaves are falling thick and fast, their message to us send.

Soon carpets of autumn shades of red, mixed with rusty brown
will lie thickly in the woods and drift into the town.

'Tis then a mood of melancholy falls upon my heart,
to know that summer's gone and winter soon will start.

It seems to be so long before the days of spring will glow,
the world will then be young again, and life will start to flow.

Rozetta Pate

AUTUMN

Autumn leaves come tumbling down, like giant snowflakes to the
ground, so silently they make no sound.
Colours yellow, brown and red, swirl gently round the garden shed,
now summer's truly put to bed.
Flowers that once flaunted gems, leafless now with cut-off stems,
no longer blooms with frilly hems.
Mornings sharp and crisp and cold, clear blue skies all bright and bold,
seed pods now will spread their gold.
Cascading leaves are in no rush, as the gardener comes to do his stuff,
with his broken handled, spiky brush.
A pile he puts for Bonfire night, bangers galore as they're set alight
and children squeal with pure delight.
As rockets shoot away up high, lighting up the night-time sky,
with plenty more in a box nearby.
Then another day is born, as we pick spent fireworks from the lawn
and once again our hearts are torn.
The months relentless marching in, summer, autumn winter, spring,
each their own surprise will bring.
But autumn has a special place, as it takes a first in the seasons race,
the others dropping down from grace.
Now it nestles firmly in, holds high its head, holds high its chin
and wears its crown with a massive grin.

Jackie Davies

AUTUMN

The first faint hint of what is yet to be
A pinkish tint upon the cherry tree
The old Virginia creeper's turning red
Around the timbers of the garden shed

Lovely in its dying, yet how beautiful
September's golden leaves
The autumn miracle

As sure as clocks and calendars
They year is growing old
Cloaks the wood in glory
Bronze, crimson, amber, gold

The fires of nature's making
The flames no man can stay
The mighty burning, blazing
That runs from day to day.

David Sheasby

THE BRAMBLE PATCH MYSTERIES

Brambles look like the work of the Devil
As hammers clanked on anvils of evil
Forging steely barbs to adorn their limbs
Just to appease the Devil's whims.

And with such antisocial habits
To rip at pelt of hapless rabbits
To claw at fur of passing cur
And pluck golden locks from intrepid fox.

With row upon row of jagged thorn
Like serried ranks of daggers drawn
As if forever fighting unseen foe
What hidden secrets are guarded so.

Are you guarding the bouquets of flowers
Within the heart of your thorny bowers
That bring joy and beauty for us to see
And abundant nectar for the bee.

Or are you guarding the black, glossy gems
Held in such regal clusters on your stems
Surely, no knave would steal these fruit
For the burden of guilt with such loot.

Yet still the treasures tempt and seduce
Those who crave the purple juice
But lo! Harken unto the spoken word
The local folk now talk of a bird.

With brazened beak that scorns the thorns
Is it the magpie, who loves to steal?
No, tis none other than the craven raven
Who has blackberry caviar with every meal.

Derek Harvey

STOP, LOOK AND LISTEN

How do you tell it's autumn?
It's getting colder we know!
But before you put on your winter dress
Take a look at what's on show.

There are trees that are silver,
Trees that are gold
And mauve of the Michaelmas daisy
Red hot pokers so straight and tall,
The holly berries so loved by all.

Take a walk in a wood
And under your feet,
The leaves go crackle and crunch,
The squirrel is going fast up a tree,
Storing his winter lunch?

Take a look in the garden,
There's old Guy Fawkes,
Piled high on the sticks for burning,
The toffee apples are being eaten
And the Catherine wheels a-turning.

Stop, look and listen,
The year's nearly gone,
We live in a world truly blessed,
Where old Mother Nature invites us now,
To put on our winter dress.

Rachel Mary Mills

OBSERVING AUTUMN

Autumn,
a sight to behold.
The leafy trees
red, yellow and gold.

Soon,
leaves will fall down.
The children will scatter
those orange and brown.

Fruit,
will be stored.
Apples and pears
join the hoard.

Sunny days,
to gladden the heart.
A feeling of sadness
as birds depart.

A chill,
in the night.
The harvest moon
shining so bright.

Enjoy,
this wondrous time.
Autumn, all its glory
while weather is fine.

Winter,
is not far away.
Enjoy these moments
make them stay.

Thora Carpenter

AUTUMN

The season of mellow changes of blended gold and brown
Where the trees are all in harmony with colours they have found.
They turn their leaves tenderly to match the growing breeze
All too soon they will lose them when the earth begins to freeze.

Conkers ripening on the trees, fall gently to the ground
Children wandering round them will wonder at what they have found.
They will prise open wide the green and prickled shell
And reveal a nut so brown and hard to crack as well.

The morning mists rise from the ground, now damp from all the dew
The snails leave their trail across the lawn and the frost brings it
                                                                into view.
The birds seem quiet now after the trees have shed their cover
As though to hide their presence they seem to whisper to one another.

When the days draw short and the nights seem long
Then we know that autumn has come along.
The weather changes and the winds start to rise,
Bringing a chill in the air that says that the flowers will not survive.

The animals too feel that hibernation must be near.
The birds leave their nests and squirrels hoard their nuts in fear.
They know that winter will too soon arrive
And without their food they will not survive.

Where once there was green, now there is brown and gold
The fields are bare and the sheep and cattle are in the fold.
The heating is on and curtains are drawn
We're all safe and sound and snug and warm.

Sheila Storr

WINTER'S ON ITS WAY

A cloudy, overcast October day,
A cold, icy wind blows drizzle and spray,
Across the fields and over the sea,
It blows round the houses and across the quay,
What unsettled, inclement autumn weather,
Blowing a gale that none can tether.
It grabs at the leaves
And pulls them off the trees,
Until the grass is covered,
The whole drive smothered,
Slowly, gradually, the wind abates and eases,
To leave a calm quietness, just a gentle breeze that freezes.

Christine Nolan

AUTUMN DUSK

As clouds reflect the dying sun
Now hidden behind the nearest hill,
Warm shades of amber, red and gold
Are tinged with mists of smoky blue,
To bring first hints of autumn chill.

There's something in this hour of dusk
That draws me irresistibly,
To wander out across the fields
And through the ancient, wild wood,
To seek a quiet reverie.

There, to commune with Nature, when
All time has lost its relevance;
Watch and absorb life's rhythm
As the earth conducts her grand affairs
With economic elegance.

The fading light reveals her store
Of fruit grown ripe in summer sun,
A scarlet flame to warm insidious
Fingerlets of dew-damp haze,
That spread through webs so carefully spun.

And now soft whisperings in the wind,
Bring news of death that lingers near,
As shadows creep on rain-dark earth,
Sad music sighs to dying day
And stirs the embers of the dying year.

Sandra L Hopwood

DEATH IN AUTUMN

Oi, you needn't try to con me,
I knew that you were coming.
Sneaking through the undergrowth,
Your sneakiness is numbing.

Moving slower than a sloth,
Yet faster than a blink.
Taking just a single soul,
You're underhand, you stink.

Soon you'll take a hundred souls
And never bat an eye.
Then you'll take a thousand more
And throw them round the sky.

You'll force the birds to fly away,
Cast shadows long and cold.
Then all that's left, you'll turn to shades,
Of orange, red and gold.

You used to take a hold of me,
Inspiring some verse.
You were a friend until I saw,
You driving summer's hearse.

Sid 'de' Knees

LEAF FALL

Some do but see the fallen leaves,
    Their royal colours thrown away,
Nor note, on each denuded twig,
    The promise of a verdant May.

Go look - asleep and closely wrapped,
    Awaiting but the call of spring,
Already formed, each fat bud shows
    Promise of life's continuing.

Kathleen M Hatton

AUTUMN TREATS

Walks in autumn sunshine,
Changing colours of the trees,
Toadstools in abundance,
Beautiful to see.

Hazelnuts and chestnuts,
Squirrels like to store,
Thinking of the months ahead,
When food is there no more.

Days of mellow fruitfulness
And crispness in the air,
A time to go on country walks
And gather nature's fare.

Ripe berries in the hedgerows,
For all who wish to eat,
For birds and animals alike,
A very welcome treat.

Dew in the morning sunlight,
On spiders webs to see,
Like precious gems they sparkle
And are there for you and me.

Lois M Pester

AUTUMN REMEMBERS

On a misty autumn day
Remembering summer has faded away.
Now evening fires burn upon the hearth
And fallen leaves rustle along the path.

Michaelmas daisies, pink and blue
Chrysanthemums tawny and sparkling with dew.
Dahlias stately in garden bed.
Fuchsias like lanterns of dusky red.

Velvet-dark nights with shooting stars
Fireworks and fun and November bonfires.
Hedgerows with berries, birds on the wing
Autumn remembers, just everything!

Meryl

SEPTEMBER SONG

The mist is lying like a veil
Over fields of corn
Low and soft and wispy
On this fine September morn.

The rising sun reflects across
Fields of misty white
Turning them to rosy pink
With early morning light.

Dark of night has gone now
Another day is dawning
Birds are singing, glad to see
The beauty of this morning.

Joan M Jones

THE AUTUMNAL CHANGES 2002

Daylight so precious, fast fading away,
Skies so blue, slowly turning to grey,
Crops fully ripened, fruit and veg too,
Farmers hurriedly gathered, had much to do.
Harvest festival thanksgiving, voices joyfully rang,
Gifts for the needy, parishioners prayed and sang.

Birds daily to sunnier climates speedily flew,
Sunny days nearly over, sunshine visits so few.
Autumn winds and rain came stronger and bolder,
The temperature dropped, suddenly it was colder,
Leaves changed to red, a golden glory and brown
Twisting and shaking, trying not to fall down.

The autumnal change yearly affects one and all,
Cold, blustery winds blow, leaves scatter and fall,
Standing naked and bare, the lonely mother tree,
Sighs for her leaves, gone with the wind, now free!
This slowing down of life, this autumn season brings,
Darkness, hibernating, rest for nature's living things.

On 26th October, hands of clocks slid back one hour
Greenwich Mean Time in UK now held the power.
Sunday 27th, roaring gales swept the country through
Havoc was created causing electrical problems too.
Previously earthquake tremors, woke folks, gave a fright,
Unexpected autumnal changes happen both daytime and night.

Rivers are rising, soon floods will slowly appear,
This is serious but seasonal, brings anxiety and fear.
Frosty nights are forecast, scenery changes to sparkling white,
Snowflakes often follow, softly falling, bring delight,
The wonders of seasonal changes are plain to see,
I wonder, did you enjoy my *autumnal changes* with me?

Stella Bush-Payne

AUTUMN THOUGHTS

Green is going, gold has come;
crunching leaves around our home
blow in heaps against the rails,
after autumn's raging gales.

As a child, I scuffed along,
kicking up the dusty throng
with youthful wonder, underfoot,
never caring that my boots
would need re-cleaning - that's the rule
for children sent 'like snails to school'.

Autumn equalled fairs and fun,
fireworks and bonfire done.
Then collecting conkers shiny,
hazelnuts and beech-mast tiny.

Brown and gold and red and yellow
for my favourite season mellow.
Leaves for pressing, leaves for drawing,
on a bitter morning, thawing
hands and feet all chilled and wet;
plenty of days till Christmas yet!

Now with adult eyes I see
the changing seasons in a tree,
from green to red and red to gold;
a lifetime's memories now I'm old.

J M Gardener

SOMETHING DIFFERENT ABOUT AUTUMN

There was something different about autumn this year
My heart it is sad for my love is not here.
Through soft spring rain and summer sky
We laughed and played, our love could not die.
With happy awakening to the day we were blessed
And wonderful nights when the sun went to rest
The silver moon and stars shining bright
While we were lovers in the night.
We were possessed with each other's charms
And I was content within his arms.
September came and leaves turned to gold,
We still were together though love had turned cold.
The winds of autumn blew dead leaves from the trees
And my lover was gone like a sigh on the breeze,
Our love it has died and away it has flown,
Now it is winter and I am alone.

Margie Fox

SUMMER'S DEATH

The late autumn sunshine
Filtered through a mackerel sky
And just for the briefest moment
Felt the ghost of summer passing by.

Then, as my eyes travelled over
The distant purple hills
I saw gathering clouds of winter there
And felt her icy chills.

As the dry leaves of autumn
Rustled over my pebbled path
I thought I heard her wintry breeze
Blow out a brittle laugh.

Then wearily, as I listened
I felt her icy fingers close
Around my summer loving heart
As her eerie spectre rose.

Arose and stretched before me
Like a serpent with icy breath,
Her eyes merrily dancing
Triumphant in summer's death.

V M McKinley

THAT AUTUMN

A valley glazed with shades of gold,
In the agate of September,
A mirrored rainbow in a stream,
That autumn, I remember.

A forest of vermilion hue,
In the cobalt of October,
The first hoar frost and crackling air,
That autumn, I remember.

The shadows stark on silver days,
In the opal of November,
The russet leaves and sunsets glow
That autumn, I remember.

The auburn of her fragrant hair,
The sweet ache of surrender,
The emerald glow within her eyes,
That autumn, I remember.

Ray Smith

SCENES OF AUTUMN

Orange, yellow, golden like the sun
Brown, russet and crimson red too
Colours of autumn
Rich and beautiful tis true.

The wind blows softly
Lifting the leaves from the trees
Falling so gracefully
Gently floating down with ease.

Apples, red and green - crisp
Waiting to be picked - at their best
Crops at the ready
Tis time for harvest.

Animals such as squirrels
Gathering nuts for their store
Tortoises and hedgehogs getting ready to hibernate
Before winter's at their door.

For people, nights are closing in
Heating and lights are going on
Time to adjust before winter comes
When we start to think -
Just where has the year gone?

Michelle Luetchford

AUTUMN LEAVES

I felt the gentle, refreshing breeze,
Rustling amongst the autumn leaves.
Lifting them as if in a dance,
Swirling and turning as they prance;
Myriad colours twirling around,
Like a carousel in a fairground.
Light and flimsy, gossamer things,
Flitting around as if with wings.
What a delight this swirling scene,
Creating magic in a sunlit dene,
The falling red, gold and brown shades,
Carpeting with autumnal colours, woodland glades.

Doris Livesey

As Autumn Fades

Fiery, glowing colours of nature all around
With autumn sunshine taking on a mellow haze,
As we tread a cautious path of leaves on the ground
Just marvelling at the beauty of these pleasant days.

Contented people carry on in special ways
Happy to be a part of nature's warming role,
Thus making much of the sun's welcome, soothing rays
Before the onset of winter takes its toll.

Discarded autumn leaves drift slowly to the ground
As the welcome, warming sunshine still appears,
The leaves that shaded well settling without a sound
And drifting underfoot, their purpose now so clear.

Sadly as they fade away, then to decompose
Returning now to earth, then finally to deplete
They lie so gently there and rest in quiet repose,
Beauty of God's earth so wonderful and complete.

As gently they begin to disappear from sight
Sadly this vision now on earth no longer seen
Who knows what role in nature, for them, is quite right
As the trees that gave them birth seem to lack esteem.

For once these graceful trees of such untold beauty
Greatly adorned with verdant leaves that served them well
Take on a weary mantle that winter now weaves,
Will they return in spring to beauty, who can tell?

As gardens still display their remaining summer flowers
That brought such lasting pleasure in the months before,
Gone are the days of light and long drawn-out hours
As with closed curtains we snuggle behind closed doors.

In sombre mood we gaze across the fields so bare
And remember them full of brightly golden corn,
Marvelling at the wealth of crops that we will share,
Do we think of farmers, their work arduously born?

Irene Grahame

NOVEMBER

November is a bitter month
When it is damp and dark and cold
We had a lovely summer
But now the year is getting old
Bonfires lift up to greet the fog
When there seems to be scarce a breeze
All nature hangs its weary head
And the trees are losing their leaves
Yet a hope rises in our hearts
The darkest hour comes before dawn
December follows November
When we remember Christ was born
He also had His darkest hour
As for us He was crucified
Then rose triumphant from the grave
Now lives, in our hearts to abide
So we praise God for November
For the carols we soon shall sing
Heralding in the New Year
With its promises of spring.

P Rock

THE FAIRY'S STORY

I'm just a little fairy upon the Christmas tree,
With lovely dress and silver wings, as pretty as can be.
They've come to put the baubles and tinsel round the tree
I might as well not be there for they're just ignoring me.
They scatter presents on the floor, they're there for all to see,
Each tied with pretty ribbons, but they don't notice me!
An assortment of Christmas lights are twisted round and round,
They stick a red one up my dress - it gets quite hot I've found.
The children dance around the tree, the lights are twinkling bright,
But they never look up to the top, I'm stuck there out of sight.
I'm wondering now what I can do, perhaps if I sit tight
The bulb will get much hotter and my dress will catch alight.
At long last they notice me as flames spread from my dress.
They use the fire extinguisher, oh what a dreadful mess.
I lay there looking so forlorn and shed a little tear,
Waiting to be washed and dressed, all ready for next year.
So as you trim your tree today, I hope you will remember,
The little fairy on the top and not a dying ember!

Vivienne Roberts

DUCKS OF CUERDEN PARK

Quack, quack, quack, quack!
I welcome you today, sir.
If I were a cat
I would certainly purr.

My friends and I saw your dog
who came down the path with friendly tread.
We waited and watched until you came
with your usual pack of bread.

We have gathered round your feet
with upturned beaks and bright eyes.
We have fought, chased and pecked our fellows,
contrary to your desires.

Quack, quack! Oh sir, you have not
fed me my fair share.
I have pecked at the bag and your shoes
to indicate my plight and despair.

Dear sir, you are so kind
to remedy this oversight.
With autumn's chill winds, your bread
will warm me through another night.

Robert Allen

EXTRA SPECIAL

This world, that God has made for me,
Is rich beyond compare,
With everything I've ever loved
And dreamed of, living there.

But now it's extra special,
In its glory and its peace,
For the autumn sun has touched it,
And its beauty is released.

The dew, that glistens on the grass,
Shimmers in the trees,
And sunlight adds a sparkle
To all the varied leaves.

The pyracantha's berries
Are orange on the wall.
The fuchsia's bells are radiant,
As the blue sky frames it all.

A proud, bright, peacock butterfly
Rests to spread its wings.
The sparrows eat the red fruits
From the hawthorn, as they sing.

My heart is full of happiness,
At this wondrous, autumn sight,
For I know God sent this vision,
To recall on winter nights.

Lorna Lea

AUTUMN

Isn't it pretty, the orange and yellow
And the greens are so many different hues
The atmosphere is peaceful and mellow
Only the leaves fall wet with dew.
A few blackbirds are playing and piping
Small birds are flitting and hiding
Before the crows send them darting
Disturbing all with their squawking
In the trees' leaves tinged with the early sun
Beautiful at 7.30 in the morning.

It's Hallowe'en and the young will have fun
Will the colours be as clear tomorrow?
Will the air be as clean and mellow?
Fireworks began last week
Tonight's the night for trick or treat.

Sylvia Shafto

THE OTHER VIEW OF AUTUMN

I hate autumn!
I hear all the poets enthusing galore
But to me all their musings are just a bore
And I'm so fed up with the leaves on the floor
I hate autumn.

I hate autumn!
The romance of the mists just passes me by,
The chill in my bones makes me want to cry
And those easterly winds bring a tear to my eye.
I hate autumn.

I hate autumn!
The night comes early, the mornings are dark,
The trees are bare when I walk in the park
And I no longer hear the song of the lark.
I hate autumn!

I hate autumn!
I don't like the cold, heavy dew on my car,
The aches in my bones make me feel below par
And I know that to winter it's not very far.
I hate autumn!

R Hannam

AUTUMN MUSIC
(I.M. Walter de la Mare)

Everything's a bit soft and hazy
The blue sky flecked with white cloud;
The sun peeps out patiently
The year is nearer to her shroud.

The months bide their time
September, October, November -
With their beautiful music-cadences
That I will ever, always remember.

Begone the dull care of winter
Listen to the larks tracing the sky,
The little, red squirrels hibernate;
Apples are ready for the pie.

And the children celebrate Hallowe'en
When there is magic abroad;
And night is lit up by lustrous stars
And the moon plays a bright chord.

Harken to the wide heavens
That whisper in the trees -
In His handiwork the great God
Makes the seasons meet at ease.

O musical voices sounding!
In the daytime; in the darkness;
Though death will wield his scythe,
I love the autumn nonetheless.

Clive Anderson

THE GIFT OF AUTUMN

Now summer's gay tints from the garden have faded,
The Earth by clust'ring leaves no longer is shaded,
The flow'r stems stand mutely, of their glory depriv'd,
The leaves of the rose-trees show that autumn's arriv'd.

The heavy-wing'd bee all his honey has taken,
And many's the bird who this land has forsaken -
Gay butterflies now no more their beauty display
And begone are the sweet scents of summer's array.

But tho' summer's nymphs deep in the Earth are sleeping,
The naiads of autumn have treasures in keeping -
The purple-starr'd daisy from Michaelmas nam'd,
The sombre chrysanthemums, sharp-scented, bronze-flam'd.

The trees they have bedecked in many-hued dress - gold
And copper, dusky-red, - magical shades that hold
The sun's heart as he glows in the soft autumn sky,
Each rare-tinted leaf an enchantment to the eye.

Ruth Shallard

OBSERVING AUTUMN

Autumn's leaves are falling now -
    tinged with red and golden brown,
A chilling note in the restless wind
    sounds harsh o'er the empty down.
Harvest moon glides regally
    through the corridors of night,
Firing the vault of Heaven
    with brilliant ghostly light.

With a sudden petulant flurry
    the menacing wind turns sour,
As if commanded by nature's magic,
    the curtains of Heaven lower,
Autumn which had walked on stage
    to a gentle warming beat,
Now stamps its mark on the shrinking land
    with frost encrusted feet.

F R Smith

Autumn Magic

Spider spin your web tonight,
Underneath the pale moonlight.
With each fragile silver thread,
Transform the dying flower bed.
So when at last your work is done,
It glistens in the autumn sun.
Heavy with the morning dew,
That brings to nature life anew.
Then looks as if some fairy hand,
Has made an insect wonderland.

Helen T Westley

NOVEMBER LAMENT

Why was I born in bleak November,
With Winter's death knell nigh?
A life should begin when cuckoos sing,
When the spring green sap is high.
While tender hedgerow leaves unfurl
And lambs frisk on the lea,
As Nature awakes to fullness -
It's then birth ought to be.

Though death is the harvest of birth,
It would be hard to die
Till the last summer flower has blown,
And swallows southwards fly,
When the withered leaves drop in the wood
And gaunt boughs rend the sky,
When cold winds moan and days are short -
November's a time to die.

Savile Sykes

SUMMER TO FALL

As summer ends most people
start to moan
One day of rain and
you hear them all groan
They don't think of the autumn
just the winter season
It's autumn I say
but they don't want to reason

Cold bright days are beginning
Leaves in the trees turn to gold
Summer flowers are dying
But the sun is still orange and bold

Enjoy the days of autumn
For they will soon be gone
Then survive through the winter months
Until the springtime sings its song.

Julie Tucker

THE COLOUR OF AUTUMN

The four seasons have a lot to behold,
Like autumn with its orange, brown and gold,
Carpet of leaves upon the ground,
When walked upon, give a crunching sound.

Trees once covered, all lush and green,
Now branches all bare, not a leaf to be seen,
No flowers showing their head,
Everything's gone to sleep instead.

They want to rest after the sun,
Rest before the winter has begun,
All the autumn colours are to stay locked in your head,
For when winter comes everything is white instead.

Dead leaves blow in the wind how they rustle,
People hurry by it's quite a bustle,
If only you would stop and look around,
At all the beautiful colours, that lay on the ground.

This carpet of colour is laid out for you,
To capture its warmth till things,
Are once again all green and new.

Rosalind Jennings

OBSERVING AUTUMN

I wander in my garden amid the autumn gloom
Water drips from branches and shades of winter loom
When, suddenly, beside the shed, I see a rose in bloom.
Its petals are unfolding as if the sun still shone
This red rose in my garden says that summer has not gone.

For me, long past my summer, when energy astounding
Gave so much looking forward and confidence abounding.
In spite of limitations in the autumn of my days
I can be encouraged in unexpected ways:
Laughter with a grandchild or a crossword puzzle done
And suddenly I know that my summer has not gone.

Joanna Young

AUTUMN

Autumn, third season of the year
Means winter time is drawing near.
Hazelnuts, acorns, conkers round
Lie upon the mud wet ground.
Trees with leaves of burnished gold
Against a sky dreary and cold,
Birds to warmer climes migrate
Hedgehogs quietly hibernate.
Down in the earth, worms wriggle and turn
Fishes snuggle in the ice cold burn,
Squirrels in their holes so deep
Prepare for nature's winter sleep,
Icy winds begin to blow
Heralding the winter's snow.

Rosalind I Caygill

AUTUMN LEAVES

The leaves are falling now it's autumn,
Leaves of yellow, brown and red,
See the beauty in the colours
As I walk and gently tread.

I love the rustle beneath my feet,
Shuffling through the leafy wood,
A memory of my childhood days,
Remembering things that were so good.

Always autumn I loved the best,
To me so magical and fun,
Imagining there were fairies around
Behind the trees and seeing none.

I'm grown up now, and still reminisce
When I walk through the wood,
Without a care in the world,
Shuffling leaves and feeling good.

Jean Lloyd-Williams

PICTURED RAIN

A pitter patter on windowpane
The heavy drops of falling rain
Two lovers' kiss with wet intent
The falling drops are Heaven sent
A misguided child dances in puddles of
Falling rain, his feet are wet, his mind is sane
A drowned rat escapes the deluge of
A terraced street, and yet no face will
He greet.
The people with umbrellas hurry by, a place
To go, a place to dry, this is no place
To stand and cry, only a place to be gone
From seek shelter and get dry
Flowers raise their petals to the sky, their
Faces wonder, they can't deny, will the downpour
Wash them dry?
The streets are deserted under grey clouds
And yet I wonder, I'm soaked now, I await
The thunder.

T McFarlane

SANTA CLAUS

S omething tells me I'm in luck,
A in't going to bed tonight,
N o siree, I'm staying up!
T onight's the night, or so I'm told,
A visitor's coming to town.
C heerful little fellow, dressed in red,
L aughs a lot and rides a sleigh,
A nswers to the name of Santa Claus.
U nderneath the Christmas tree,
S anta's leaving a present just for me.

Annette Murphy

OUTLOOK UNSETTLED

Rain silvers its way down cloud hung string
for the wind to wrap round the parcel of Earth,
which contains our present of forthcoming spring
to give colour, scents and blossom around its girth.

Rain trickles down roofs into rusty gutters,
seeps with oozing drips into lumps of leaves;
smears grubby trails down the flaking shutters,
drawing a misty grey curtain through leafless trees.

Each raindrop on hitting the windowpane
falls with a tail that marks its end;
it will leave a puddle which may dry with a stain,
it will make leaves heavy that the wind will bend.

When snow's mat is wiped hard under our feet
the cold penetrates and the soil will freeze;
then raindrops fall as a stinging sleet,
scattering nature's pearls onto Christmas trees.

Anoraks and umbrellas come to our defence
when storms come to pelt us with a constant flow;
to drench us seemingly in an endless sequence,
yet the old folks prefer it to the slippery snow!

Dennis Marshall

SEASONAL AFFECTED DISORDER

Where now the lass in flowing blouse,
Who skipped among the summer flowers.
Green leaves are turning golden now,
The days get shorter hour by hour,
Chill winds will come to strip the boughs,
And tall dark clouds like granite towers,
Depress, and make the strongest cower.
The weakest, winter will devour,
And vaunt it's cold impassive powers,
With freezing sleet and snowy showers.
While overhead the sparkling plough,
And hungry, screeching, searching owl,
Will give no thought for summer flowers,
Or lass who skipped in flowing blouse.

R Bowhill

AUTUMN

When the trees are full of colour
And their leaves are painted bright
When autumn leaves are falling
In parks it's quite a sight
The squirrels gather nuts
To store for winter time
Animals prepare to hibernate
In comfort most sublime
The days are growing shorter
The nights are dark and long
The weather's getting colder
The warmth of summer gone.

Catherine Armstrong

AUTUMN

Golden leaves, all crisp and dry
Drift down in the fiery sun.
Smoke from bonfires spirals up
Now day is almost done.
For this is the time when plants die down,
As nature prepares for sleep
And creatures who need some protection from cold
Burrow down in the compost heap.

The conkers shine and the nuts turn brown
Berries in the hedgerow glow red,
Nature's provisions for those who hoard
Before they go to bed.
The frosts will come, when the days get short
And winter's chill arrives.
Yet God gives them time to forage and store
What is needed to stay alive.

The trees loom grey in the evening mist,
As dampness touches the ground.
The shadows lengthen, in the autumn chill
Listen, there is no sound.
Soon the hunters emerge, as night time falls,
To seek an evening meal.
The eye of the fox has an amber glint
Aware of what's there to steal.

But hark to the thunder of horses' hooves,
The call of the hunter's horn
As the fox in turn is target for the kill,
In the mists of an autumn morn.

Pamela Carder

AUTUMN

I loved autumn leaves when I was young
As they dried upon the ground
I would kick them on my way to school
They made a lovely sound
But that's all changed, now I am old
It only makes me sad
To think of happy days gone by
And all the fun I had.

Autumn brings Guy Fawkes and Hallowe'en
For a child that's a lot of fun
And then there follows Christmas
Well, I'd rather have the sun
For somehow Christmas is not the same
When you are just the one
It's hard to feel full of good cheer
And join in all the fun.

So spring is really more my style
It cheers me up no end
When nature starts to come alive
And summer's round the bend.

June Davies

Autumn Slumbers

The golden leaves fall off the trees,
Drift slowly to the ground.
My breath comes out in icy puffs,
And nothing makes a sound.

The last few birds are huddled up
To try and beat the chills.
The flocks of sheep and herds of cows
Have all gone from the hills.

The tiny forest animals
Are tucked up safe asleep.
Still I wouldn't want to wake them,
So quietly I creep.

It's so early in the morning,
And summer's really past.
There's Hallowe'en and Bonfire Night
Now autumn's here at last.

Kaz

AUTUMN WALK

I walked beneath the autumn sun
My heart softly beating as I gazed at the sky
The trees were shedding their leaves
Preparing to sleep through the winter's breeze
Fairies dancing high above
for soon the snow would cover the leaves

Leaves fall around my head
Telling me it's time for bed
For soon the winter snow will come
Towards the spring we will run
Hand in hand we walk the path
That takes us home together at last
For in my heart I know for sure
That winter will bring us happiness and joy

Spring has gone the autumn is here
So now is time for rest
To look upon the face of my love
In our cosy nest
Though winds will blow
Snow may fall
Darkness cover the land
As I sleep my dreams will be
Of an autumn spent with thee.

White Knight

LATE AUTUMN

The leaves are now falling
Falling down fast
From most of the trees
They are the last

They would rest beneath
In a quiet way
But high winds will come
And blow them away

Outside the windows
Once more they'll flitter
- Playthings for birds -
But for people just litter

Meanwhile the trees
Washed down by rain
Long for a new spring
To blossom again.

Tony Gyimes

SET FARE FOR AUTUMN

Write a poem about autumn they said
So picturesque and appealing
Tell us about all its joys,
Set our senses reeling.

Sorry, don't do 'scudding clouds'
'Cobwebs like delicate lace'
Let's think bye bye to grockel crowds
And talk about feeding our face.

Ignore the drifts of heather
Bronzing and crimson leaves
Let's eat to greet the weather,
Fish and chips and mushy peas.

Yes, curling waves are a picture
Underbellies flecked with foam
But focus on toasted crumpets
Dripping butter, back at home.

Winter's on the horizon
Like the squirrels let's prepare
Be ready for hibernation
With wholesome and succulent fare.

Forget cold ham and salads
Chilly, frozen sweets
Think apple pie and custard
Spotted dick and other treats.

Dumplings light and fluffy,
Lemon pancakes by the score
Bacon sarnies with HP sauce
Curries and chillies galore!

Yes, there's a hint of frost in the air
And the moon wears her autumnal gown
But me, I'm preparing for winter,
Stocking up on the best food in town.

Vera Morrill

THE AUTUMN OF LIFE

From green to red,
Gold and brown,
The leaves on the trees
Come tumbling down.
On the ground,
Wrinkled and dried,
They lie for children
To kick aside.

My hair has changed
To grey from brown.
Parts of my body
Come tumbling down.
My skin has become
Wrinkled and dried.
In the autumn of life
I'm kicked aside.

Jackie Barker-Smith

NOVEMBER MORNING

Smoking chimneys over blue slate rooftops
Moving grey cloud distant brightness sight
Overcast and dismal Thursday morning
Remaining remnants of a rain shed night.

November morning leafless trees in distance
Silhouettes stand motionless and stark
Pigeons, swirling smoke around greyness
Haunting prelude to the early dark.

Lifeless stillness reigns at rooftop level
Looking down on dullness damp and gloom
Cloud covered sun through haze has won its battle
Breaks through to light the darkness of my room.

Christopher S Mills

Autumn

All around us varied tints
Colourings which strongly hint
That autumn now is here to stay,
With mellowed hues, till wintry days
Descend upon us with their chill
Then naught but barren field and hill.

In abundance leaf will fall,
Blown by keen winds over all,
Mulch at last into a ground,
Seeming lifeless all around.

Cocooned safely there below
A future bounty waits to grow,
Dormant until spring is near
And signs of life again appear.

Autumn bounty makes us smile
But only for that brief, brief while,
Fulfilling Mother Nature's plan
Just part of her great, yearly span.

Ellen Thompson

MISTS OF AUTUMN

Mists of autumn round trees,
Trying to keep them warm,
As they are without leaves
And must come to no harm.

Wildfowl make mournful cries,
As they know winter's near.
They must make their goodbyes
Before weather cold and seer.

Stillness hangs on the air;
A pungent scent prevails.
Smoke and mist a murky pair,
Yet they make autumn veils.

J Millington

A Child's Autumn

Autumn, the most enchanting of seasons.
If you're a child there are many reasons
To celebrate. New class, maybe new school:
A change of uniform is always cool.
In early weeks, there's often good weather.
On lighter evenings you get together,
Just like summer. There are leaves to scuff, conkers to play.
Then it's half-term, and you're home all day.

Schools go back, and so do the clocks.
It's darker, wetter, colder: warm coat; thick socks.
Before you know it, there's Hallowe'en.
You've never lived until you've been
Trick or treating. With pumpkin lantern, spooky story,
And anything ghostly, ghoulish or gory.
No time to recover, soon it's Bonfire Night.
A wondrous, magical evening of light.

Just when you think the good things have gone,
Look around, and you'll see everyone
Has Christmas on their mind.
Shopping trips galore until you find
Perfect presents. There are cakes to bake;
Cards and decorations to make;
Concerts to plan; carols to hum.
It's fab being a child in the autumn.

Valerie Catterall

OBSERVING AUTUMN

Hoar frost greets the rising morn,
Crystalline dewdrops bedeck the lawn,
Cobwebs on hedgerows like old lace,
The beauty of autumn showing face,
The delicate briar rose has died,
Along with honeysuckle by her side,
Trees that once were green and fresh,
Now slipping into autumn dress,
The watery sun's rays shining down,
Enhancing leaves of red, yellow and brown,
Country lanes thick with leaves,
Brutally torn from sleepy trees,
Soft wet mist over pastures lie,
Skeletal trees with their mournful sigh,
Droplets on each lingering rose,
Shimmering like jewels midst autumn's throes,
Molten skies of the setting sun,
Like a wash of colour left to run,
Frost upon the woodland path,
Log fires burning in the hearth,
Bulbs imprisoned in hardened ground,
Waiting for spring to come around,
Like a tired maiden closing her eyes,
The last leaf of autumn finally dies.

Monica Wood

SCENES OF AUTUMN

Autumn brings ripe berries . . .
Summer's gown grows pale;
Robin sings a sweeter song
With Autumn's tawny veil;
Leaves turn gold and russet-brown
Then fall . . . in a sudden gale;
White horses ride the rough, wild waves,
Small boats reef down their sails.
Yet the Autumn sun still strongly burns
In a sky of azure blue,
And mellow fruit hangs on the bough . . .
Of gold and scarlet hue.
The moors are clothed in heather -
White clouds race overhead,
A fox slinks through the undergrowth . . .
Watchful rabbits have all fled.
Dahlias flaunt their vivid colours
From cottage garden beds,
Their faces fresh with morning dew
As the sun climbs overhead.
Wreathes of pearly mist are lifting
From a sea as pale as milk,
Seabirds drift with the early tide
On a surface - smooth as silk.
When the frost lies thick
On the meadow grass
And the moon is at the full,
Log fires scent the evening air -
Crisp . . . and cold . . . and still.
Though it's sad to watch bright Summer die,
The changing scenes of Autumn
Will stir the heart . . .
Whilst delighting the eye.

Elizabeth Amy Johns

Autumn

Yes, summertime is past; the long, long days
And liquid warmth are over for this year;
The wind is strong, howe'er the sun doth blaze,
And we can tell that winter's drawing near.

The winds have stripped the leaves from off the trees.
The few left hanging there are red and brown,
Orange and yellow; and so weak are these
The merest puff will send them fluttering down.

But midst the sombre hues of red and brown
Some leaves still green do suddenly appear
For promise that though winter's snow come down
Another summertime will soon be here.

Jillian Mounter

ODE TO RAIN

I like it when it rains
When the wind blows hard against the windowpane.
The sound of water rushing along the gutters
Loosening the leaves so down they flutter.

I like it when it pours
Like a waterfall down the windowpane.
When it comes with thunder and with lightning
Flashing and crashing can be frightening.

I like being indoors when it rains
Pressing my face against the windowpane
Safe and looking out, it's quite exciting
Call me weird but to me it's strangely inviting.

I like being outside when it rains
Looking back at the windowpane.
Hearing the pitter-pat on my brolly
Splashing in puddles feeling jolly.

I like the feeling of rain on my skin
Dripping off my nose and chin.
Getting soaked right through my clothes
That's my secret, no one knows.

I really like it when it rains.

Elizabeth Morton

AUTUMN RAIN

Sunday morning all chores done,
We woke with a smile to find no sun.
The room was dark and the sky was grey,
Long overdue was the wet windy day.

Dressing gowns on and kettle boiled.
We snuggled and cuddled both of us coiled,
Like two little hamsters in a nest,
We sipped hot tea and felt our best.

The dog he sighed, as he heard us talk.
Not very patient as he awaited his walk.
So wrapped up well, in hats and coats
We ventured into weather for boats.

Off we trekked through dancing trees,
Which cheered the rain that nourished their leaves.
Then alongside a stream fast in flow,
That flooded the ground where the plants would grow.

We headed home through the misty, wet town
Shielding our faces with hoods held down.
As we opened our door the wind gave a last howl
And the dog he replied with a spotty dog growl.

Coats off and all rubbed dry,
We looked out of the windows, which seemed to cry.
Then we settled down into our cosy nest,
And once again we felt at our best.

Robert Simpson

AUTUMN

The colours of nature now autumn is here.
Are a joy to behold in the crisp dry air.
Yellow, brown, gold and red,
With the still warm sunshine overhead.

The misty mornings are damp and cold,
The fog drifts around in a ghostly shroud,
The spider's webs hang heavy with dew,
And sparkle like jewels when the sun breaks through.

Potatoes, carrots, onions and beet,
Stored for the winter for us to eat.
Apples and pears are put aside,
The squirrels hide nuts so that they can survive.

Winter will soon be on its way,
So make the most of every day,
Thank God for the autumn, He created it all,
The rotating seasons, spring, summer, winter and fall.

V Hankins

SEEDLINGS

Today, at Quaker meeting
Our younger children's class
Had fun with talk of trees and seeds
And growing things in jars of glass

What tree gives us the conker?
Yes, you can have one when you go
What is alfalfa seed
Does anybody know?

Now, draw somebody sowing seeds
And add a little glue
Shake on some lentils, or some rice
Yes, a nice sunflower will do

As we have talked of seeds today
Do you know what you grew from?
A long and busy silence . . .
Then: 'From birth!' said Tom.

Joseph McGarraghy

MELLOW SEASON

Summer is gone and over
In the grass no more clover.
Flowers with a fragrance were there
With sunshine and a glorious air.
The season we so loved is past
Such an occasion is never to last.
As beautiful colourful leaves begin to fall
Gigantic shapes of trees appear so tall.
Now winter will soon be along
As we hear a joyful Christmas song.
Awaiting the appearance of flakes of snow
Whether they will fall we do not know.
We look now ahead with glee
Wondering what another year is to be.
A time of cold, darkness but mellow fruitfulness
Therefore a time to give thanks and bless.

Iris E Weller

AUTUMN IN THE PURBECKS

The sun's hot rays are fading,
The days are shortening now,
As pears and apples ripen
On heavy laden bough.

The ferry still goes back and forth
Between Sandbanks and Shell Bay,
But its decks are far less crowded
Than on a summer's day.

From Studland's sandy beaches
The tourists are long gone;
Taking memories of lazy days
Spent idling in the sun.

At Swanage you'll find the beach huts
Are locked up until next year.
The children have gone back to school
There's no one paddling here.

The ruins of Corfe Castle
Are shrouded in a mist.
Dark tales of strife and battle
Are all that now exist.

And down on Wareham's Quay
One can find a parking space
No longer filled by strangers
But instead a familiar face.

It's peaceful here in Purbeck
Now the visitors have gone
For summer days are ended
And autumn has begun.

A M Craven

Prelude To Winter

The last rays of summer are all but gone
as the year advances on.
The trees that once were verdant green
now change and take on autumn's theme,
rich red and russet become their attire
with colours of gold and blazing fire.

The sun still bright yellow, its heat fading fast,
a chill on the ground, fresh iced dew on the grass.
The hedgerows have berries of blood-red and black
and birds eat their fill before winter comes back.

A sky though still blue has a much paler hue
streaked with white and grey cloud
as the sky starts to crowd,
and those birds that migrate
head for much warmer states.

As the chilled autumn rain
soaks the ground once again,
with a musty peat smell
from were last year's leaves fell,
fertilising the hopes
of a new season's growth.

It's a time of great plenty
as nature winds down,
where the last falls of summer
will cover the ground,
this season of richness, its colours so grand,
that time before winter envelopes the land.

Michael Close

SEASCAPE

Deep golden red are the sunsets over Bigbury Bay
reflecting light over land and sea with an ethereal glow,
whether on cliff top or Bolt Tail, to see the sun at its best
before it dips into oblivion in the west.

While by morning a mist covers Bolt Tail
as burnt orange bracken glows,
and reddish brown rocks are a background
to a sliver of beach below.

Tides come and go as tides will
leaving slippery weed on shoreline,
but above 'Inner Hope' or picnic on beach
Bolt Tail is never out of reach.

So through a tunnel of trees
to the green fields beyond
where spiders spin cobwebs of silver around
and mushrooms are gathered and blackberries too,
of course this in autumn with grasses of dew.

Gone are the fishermen of yesteryear
whose brawny arms did haul countless
pots of crab and lobster
a livelihood done well!

Alas we leave 'Hope' with memories serene,
and then like Bolt Tail our eyes mist up
in this sanctuary of peace.

Hazel Sheppard

AUTUMN DAYS

The smell of autumn fills the air
Berries ripen everywhere
Now the leaves are falling too
Wonderful colours of every hue
Floating gently to the ground
Big shiny chestnuts can now be found
Children hunt them and shout with glee
Running home as fast as can be
Finding string to put the 'conkers' on
Thinking - this year I'll be the champion.

Doris Lilian Critchley

WILD, WILD WINDS

Tranquil autumn days, sunny and warm
Nature spreading its glory in colourful charm
Shorter days, cosy fires, curtains drawn -
Then all of a sudden came the storm.
Wild, wild winds attacking all in its path
Trees bending and twisting, caught in the wind's wrath.
Variegated leaves blown wildly to the ground
Swirling into drifts and wet soggy mounds.
With the wild, wild winds came pouring rain
Lashing down so hard, too much for the drains
Flooding rivers and roads, holding up traffic
Trees uprooted, causing danger and havoc.
Electricity wires down, no lights night or day
Used torches and candles to light our way.
Violent storms at sea, a danger to all
Enormous waves crashing over the sea wall.
The abating storm left destruction in its wake
After the wild, wild winds came tranquillity and peace.

Lorna June Burdon

Autumn Shades

Season of red and gold and brown;
Of harvest-time and Hallowe'en.
When squirrels hunt for nuts to hide
And children squeal with joy as they run
To find the brown and shiny conkers from the chestnut trees.
Autumnal gales whip up the seas
Lashing the coast with fierce and cruel waves
Leaving behind seaweed-strewn beaches
Where gulls strut looking for crabs and other delicacies.
Great trees are felled and debris lies about
And leaves, brown and withered, fly around like whirling dervishes,
Forming huge piles in gardens and in parks,
Warm beds for sleepy hedgehogs and the timid mouse.
Rivers that flowed gently in the summertime
Are swollen with the heavy rain, and now
Rush noisily to the waiting sea,
And reservoirs, depleted by the summer drought,
Are full again.
The first sharp frost, after a clear and starry night,
Makes tiny skating rinks of puddles in the lane
And spiders' webs are decked with sparkling jewels
As they hang in the nearby hedge that is
Ablaze with blackberry, hip and haw,
Food for the hungry blackbird and the thrush.
The sun, divested of its summer heat,
Gives gentle warmth to the earth below.
'All is safely gathered in,' the people sing,
And bring their 'harvest' into churches through the land.
Plums, apples and a sheaf of corn lie by the altar steps
(And choirboys eye them with a greedy stare!)
This is a time of thankfulness and peace,
Of taking stock before the winter closes in.
Enjoy this autumn time, the changing hues of nature all around,
And be content, and be content.

Ann Linney

AUTUMN

Sunlight glinting thro' gold-brown leaves
Whispering windmills and windblown sheaves
Harvest home and orchard fruits
Autumn colours soft and mute

Dawn dew on a silvery thread
Enhancing the beauty of a spider's web
Fallen leaves on the forest floor
Squirrels gather nuts to eat and store

Bulrushes by the water's edge
Indian summer and a stolen pledge
Birds gather in squabbling flocks
Ready to migrate before winter's frost

Golden hay and bales of straw
English landscape to the core
Autumn days and autumn nights
Softening the way for winter's flights

Sylvia Partridge

ODE TO AUTUMN

There they stand in colours of yellow and red
Having changed out of wearing only green.
The days are sunny still, no dread
Of cooler days yet to be seen.

But, then they start to shed,
These lovely colours to the ground
Making others come to spread
These now grubby colours all around.

So, mostly now, there they stand
Completely bare in the coming cold,
Though still looking very grand
Whilst acknowledging the autumn's hold.

They know that, without a doubt,
The time soon will come
When, again in green they venture out,
To precede once more the rich colours of autumn.

Joan McLoughlin

Autumn

Autumn sneaks in silently when unexpected,
One day it's sunshine, warmth, and sunny skies,
Then, suddenly, as if it's mis-directed,
The air grows cold, and summer sunshine dies.
A dull and stronger wind the sky unleashes,
And mists enclose the morning air in dampening grip,
And rain, a once frequent visitor, increases,
The days are dark and short, and drainpipes drip.
The threatening sky is filled with tales of witches,
Warlocks, wizards and werewolves - Hallowe'en,
With all its ghosts and terrifying pitches
Of 'trick or treat', and pumpkins join the scene.
The trees, now clad in many coloured coats,
Change slowly, leafless frames stand stark and bare,
As nature, with her seasonal teasing, gloats
Over a numbing beauty, strange and rare.
Gloves suddenly appear to warm the stinging fingers,
Toes tingle, noses turn to brightest red,
The healthy stay outside, whilst shallow sunshine lingers,
The others wish that they could stay in bed.
And yet the season brings its many treasures,
Football, crisp air, and warming firelight glow,
Harvest, cold winds, contrasting fireside pleasures,
Bazaars and fireworks in a glittering show.
Food, friends, and fellowship portray the season,
With board games, dancing, indoor pleasures to the fore.
An inner warmth that grows and gives the reason
We love the autumn season more and more.

Jack Scrafton

AUTUMN COLOURS

As I look out of my window,
This is what's seen,
Leaves yellow, orange and brown,
And yet, some are still green.

A willow's fronds from her branches hang,
Gently swaying in the breeze,
The hues and shades are many,
How the autumn colours please.

The sky is grey and dismal,
The air so cold and damp,
But the autumn colours are glowing,
Like that of a bright shining lamp.

As I stand and watch the leaves,
Giving their last glorious show,
The wind blows much harder,
And some have to let go.

Other trees are standing,
With leaves so colourfully bold,
But they too will very soon,
Have to give up their hold.

Bright red rose hips,
On the briar rose,
The evergreens are bending,
Standing in defiant pose.

The autumn colours are here,
To let everyone know,
That winter is coming,
Maybe even some snow.

Christine Cyster

Autumn

In autumn the leaves from the trees fall and lie everywhere,
As you walk the paths you see the trees standing all stark and bare.
You see the council worker as he sweeps the leaves away,
Leaves of brown and gold lie in a heap as you walk by on your way.

Yes, autumn is the time when the trees do shed their leaves,
The months after summer and before winter as time as usual flees.
It seems the earth prepares for winter in the autumn days,
The cold days that the squirrel has gathered his nuts
For when he wakes from his winter laze.

I'd much rather have autumn than winter's cold, dark days,
For as you get older it gets harder in those cold, harsh days.
No I don't mind autumn with its many leaves along the way,
Give me leaves falling around me on an autumn day.

R W Cummings

Autumn

Autumn arrives with paint on a breeze,
Turning green leaves red and gold,
Winds assist in dismantling trees,
Soon to brace up to the cold.
Kicking and crunching the leaves under feet,
A sound to enjoy when out strolling,
Each season holds beauty, to the eye a treat,
Sky, sea and land ever rolling.

Monica D Buxton

Autumn Reflections

Bursting blooms to burnished boughs,
fresh greens to russet browns.
Bright blues to graceful greys,
sunbright shows to golden glows.
Sassy strawberries to plump plums,
bristling blades to straw clumps.
Peeling petals to lolling leaves,
fun-filled fairs to harvest harmonies.
Carefree cries become sager sighs,
heat hazes merge to misty mazes.
And summer to autumn subtly arrives.

So summer sheds its fussy frills
and autumn assumes its muted mantle.
Now, ripeness boasts promise to fulfil
and autumn's riches come with its example.
As sun-kissed blossoms stop prancing
and berry bunches bend for picking,
as nature folds its fluttering wings
and lightness more to darkness brings,
we can mellow with our autumnal sun,
retreat to what now can be done,
rekindle fires and friendships gone
and reflect, if we, like autumn,
are moving on.

Rosalia Campbell Orr

Swallows Gather

Swallows gather round the barn
Like clouds that bring a summer storm,
Darkening the sky.
But something different in the way they fly.
Graceful glide curtailed to anxious dart,
Watching for the first one to depart,
The leader of the long flight south.
Below
A woman, standing in the sun,
Feels a twinge of sadness,
Another summer
Done.

Pam Hatcher

THE AUTUMN BOY

The Close lay silent in the autumn sun
Leaves tidily swept - a job well done.
A boy came along and started to play
And ruffled and scuffled them every way

Then threw them about and shouted with glee.
'Til a woman came out and wanted to see
Who was the cause of this tyranny.

She shouted in anger; the boy swiftly fled
From the crunched crinkly leaves lying so dead.

A mischievous wind awakened their trance
They whirled and they twisted in magical dance.
Faster and faster they spun in the air
The broom and its owner looked on in despair
Then turned around and went away
Vowing to sweep another day.

But I can never forget the joy
Of the prancing feet of the 'Autumn Boy'.

Margo Mallett

WINTERTIME

I sit alone by the warm log fire,
I feel content as I watch 'Songs Of Praise'
And listen in amazement to the choir.
They sing 'Ave Maria' with tender sweetness,
They sing it in all its entirety and completeness,
I doze, I feel at peace and serene,
I awaken, as suddenly my cat graces the scene,
Up she jumps upon my knee,
Mewing with persistence, wanting her tea.
I go to the kitchen and feel a chill,
It is sleeting outside and there's frost on my window sill.
My letter box rattles, the wind wuthers nigh,
The trees sway and they seem to sigh.
But I count my blessings on this cold winter's night,
And remember Christ's saying,
'I am the light'.

Margaret Andrews Sherrington

BRAMBLE JELLY!
(Dedicated to fond memories of my mother)

When I was a boy my mother made jam,
In autumn, the favourite was bramble
To the bushes and lanes on the hills where I lived
With a bucket or two I would ramble
A favourite spot was old Tinkers Loane
Where travellers camped way langsyne
The brambles down there were black, fat and lush
The jelly they made was divine

The combination one red and two black
To make the jam set in the pan
The berries were lush with autumn-like tints
The spiky spears ripping your hand
The birds in the bush you'd see as you picked
While rabbits would make their escape
It was fun, it was free, it was brambles for me,
For autumn I just couldn't wait

The berries and sugar would boil in a pan;
My mother would stir with a spoon
Then take the black gunge and strain
Through a bag of muslin in her cooking room
She potted the jelly in empty glass jars
A piece of greasepaper on it
An old autumn ritual that I hold dear
Inside it my mother is lit

Roy A Millar

AUTUMNAL STROLL

The jewelled cobweb of a spider
    Glistens in the October light
Frosted by the overnight chill,
Leaves crackle under your feet
    As you amble between trees
Barren of foliage, now deadly still.

A silence prevails, the way ahead
    Appears tired and dreary,
Waiting perhaps for warmer days,
The verge cut back uncaringly
    Looks untidy and wanton
In the mystical autumn haze.

Thickets of hawthorn and bramble
    Are reflected upside down
On a smooth ice-covered pool,
Whilst outside this isolated copse
    Foxhounds and riders gather
To end life in manner so cruel.

The faint shadow of the footbridge,
    Ripples on the cold surface
Of the stream trickling below,
Rooks scatter as your footfalls
    Echo on the wooden crossbeams
Creaking menacingly as you go.

The path meanders away lazily
    Rising uphill towards a clearing
Where once the bluebells swayed,
Now, no trace of fragrance lingers,
    The last foxgloves have wilted
Bitten by nature's frosty raid.

In the distance the old water mill
    Derelict from many years past
Stands like a ghost in the night,
The fence once white has faded
    The road overgrown without use
An artist's picture, or an ugly sight.

I leave the woods to their solitude
    It has beauty, enchantment, life
Forever changing its tableau,
She conceals away her inner secrets,
    Revealing her wisdom to those
Who can sense her mood anew.

George S Johnstone

ODIUM TO WINTER

Raw winter with your slurried skies
And freezing gusts of wind,
We *did* enjoy blue summer's warmth:
Thus doing, did we sin?

Are you upset we all prefer
The azure blue to grey?
And fly away to 'summer' climes
A winter's break away!

What makes you think we all enjoy
Your being such a clown!
'Round gusty corners you await
So you can blast us down.

What about your dangerous pranks
Perversely played with glee,
Ice thinly spread on tarmac's black
You *know* we'll never see!

When boorishly you heap those piles
Of snow against our door,
And freeze car-locks maliciously
Of course these we deplore!

And even when, at Christmas time
You know we'd love you white,
More likely then you'll give us fog
In *chaos* you delight!

And when we hear you've laid your snow
On Scotland's Aviemore,
With joy we take our skis along
Arriving . . . as you thaw!

Of course it's summer we prefer
The other seasons too.
No point that we should hide the fact
We hate the likes of you!

Ron Hails

As Summer Turns To Autumn

A late August sky laden with snowy-white ruffles and
                                               silvery blue streams
Like a great ship floating peacefully to a land of distant dreams
Larks and linnets sing farewell as migrating swallows poise to fly
Nature's perfect picture to remember forever as years go by
Soft summer rain has made the countryside green and lush
The trees, hills and valleys are whispering hush
Let's cling to our emerald mantles, so beautiful and bold
Autumn winds will soon change them to a carpet of copper and gold
Strawberry-blond cornfields, full and ripe, seem to stretch for miles
As they perform a breathtaking dance of last summer smiles
Magnificent silver salmon leap to escape fishermen's dreaded hooks
While busy brown trout glide swiftly through streams and
                                               babbling brooks
Dazzling shades of sunny yellow, leafy green and bright sky blue
Showing signs of fading fast to autumn's ochre, brown and russet hue
The waning summer sun struggles bravely with September
                                               morning mist
Then meekly surrenders to the powerful grasp of autumn's firm fist.

Angela Moore

CONKER TIME

In autumn time dead leaves begin to fall
From branches of horse chestnut trees,
Which through the summer shaded one and all
Accompanied by summer's gentle breeze.

And at this harvest season of the year
The chestnut trees now give up their fruits,
Enveloped in a hardened casing green
Which split upon their contact with the roots.

Then are revealed the dark brown shiny seed
So prized by children of whatever age,
Who have impatiently awaited for their fall
And brought back childhood memories to the sage.

The shiny seeds are then baked in an oven hot
Or steeped in vinegar for many days,
The ancient folklore of hardening horse chestnut shells
Has been through times long gone a secret maze.

Then proudly threaded on a length of string
Now is the time to find out what the prize is worth,
They bash against opponents' conkers with a thud
Until opponents' conkers shatter to the earth.

Yet through the years we seem to have gone soft
Indeed I think do-gooders have gone bonkers,
This ancient sport played by children down the ages
How dare they put a ban on games of conkers?

David A Garside

Overcast

The seasons are no longer warm,
and I can feel the brewing of a storm,
the clouds are crying, starting to mourn.
Doesn't matter what we do or say,
each and every hour of a single day,
we slip further and further away.
Where we're going no one really knows,
who can guess which way the storm blows,
so all the windows and doors I try to close.
If you decide to leave me today,
don't turn back and try to stay,
as I'll be walking the other way.
If you search all of your mind,
I think you will try to find,
a sanctuary of a different kind.
I wish it was just a passing phase,
but the storm is blowing too many ways,
leaving us with a bleak sky, a cloudy daze.
I know you like this time of year,
but it is so cold standing here,
and the distant horizon is clear.
So I'm leaving the scene of the crime,
and it's definitely for good this time,
and I can't escape this feeling of mine.
It's almost like I've won first prize,
a feeling that I just can't disguise,
as I'm leaving behind these autumn skies.
I turn from you and you turn from me,
and I hear one last bolt of electricity,
then it rained smiles as I walked free.

Dale Mullock

OCTOBER RAIN

When the first October rain starts to fall,
The memories in me, they do recall,
Then turning back the pages in my mind,
Thoughts of you and me there I find.
Like under a bus shelter when we went to town,
Where we sat and watched the rain come down.
When the thunder rolled across an angry sky,
You said you'd love me till you die.
When you kissed me and whispered, 'I cannot let this moment pass.'
And with your finger you wrote upon the shelter glass.
Just for me will you do one thing?
My darling, will you wear my wedding ring?
And let it be written in the rain and in my heart,
That we two now will never part.
Then with joy in my heart and tears in my eyes,
'Yes darling, yes,' I cried.
'I'll be glad and honoured to be your wife,
And walk beside you throughout life.'
You will never know the thoughts that are in my head,
So darling, slumber softly in your bed.
Loving memories that are stirred up once again
By the falling of the first October rain.

A P Starling

A Rainy Day

Till the nights draw nigh, and lights are low
Keeping ourselves warm, by the fireside glow
When the heavens open, and the rain heavily falls
As I put pen to paper, till the night falls

Watching the raindrops, beating on the windowpane
While the thunder roars, and lightning strikes again
The wind's so boisterous as it speeds by
Hailing its worst, whistling, from the chimney high

Listening to people saying, 'What a miserable day
Rain, rain come back another day, and just go away'
What is the use, for the next day could be bright
The sun could be shining, to bring out its light

As I look outside, and see the rain falling
The dark clouds have no sign, of even breaking
As the late eve draws nigh, the winds stop hailing
The thunder starts to cease, no sign of lightning

The evening is calm and still once more
So *far* away is the rain, as it fails to pour
Just thank the Lord, whatever the weather
Even if we are on our own, He will be our protector

Even when the rains are heavy, and the thunder roars
God will be there, when you call Him yours
The wet misery of the day, may bring the special atmosphere
Till the night falls, you may feel no fear

Jean P McGovern

WRITTEN IN THE RAIN

Six months had passed from April
It was hot and sticky *and* no rain still,
September came and went
The heat, burning sun, would not relent,
Even the leaves stayed green,
No reds or browns, colours to be seen.
Suddenly late on one October night
I had just gone to bed, put out the light
When a small sound, a pitter-patter came
I could not believe it, had I heard rain?
Yes, by gosh! Then a huge splosh!
I crept to look out of my window
Thank God! At last 'rain' ho! Ho! Ho!
The flower pots were dull and dry
By morning they would change
From being filled with dull, dry plants
At last they would grow, rain at last
Better than water from the tap
The 'real stuff' from the sky makes them snap
Back into colour and now they grow
They have waited all summer to glow.

B Clark

POOL OF TEARS

A rolling, tumbling, growling sound,
shudders the air and shakes the ground.
A stabbing incandescent light,
forks through bloated clouds with white.
A scattered mist of raindrops form,
and soon become a raging storm.
The tempest's soaking drops so cool,
enjoin to make a shallow pool.
Come lift your face to feel the rain
and wash away the tears and pain.
Your empty heart, now swept with showers,
will bloom and fill with love and flowers.
The rain will flush away your fears,
now turn,
and leave,
that pool of tears.

Ray Smith

THE STORM

The wind glides through the trees, making an eerie sound
Picking up speed, whipping up leaves off the ground
A blizzard of leaves blotting out the view
Animals hide from this all engulfing brew
Branches bend and snap under this unleashed power
More and more destruction, hour by hour
Then as if by magic, the storm abates
This deafening silence on your nerves grates
The invisible destroyer has breathed its last
Its moment of glory has finally passed.

A Howells

ANCHOR BOOKS
SUBMISSIONS INVITED
SOMETHING FOR EVERYONE

ANCHOR BOOKS GEN - Any subject, light-hearted clean fun, nothing unprintable please.

THE OPPOSITE SEX - Have your say on the opposite gender. Do they drive you mad or can we co-exist in harmony?

THE NATURAL WORLD - Are we destroying the world around us? What should we do to preserve the beauty and the future of our planet - you decide!

All poems no longer than 30 lines.
Always welcome! No fee!
Plus cash prizes to be won!

Mark your envelope (eg *The Natural World*)
And send to:
Anchor Books
Remus House, Coltsfoot Drive
Peterborough, PE2 9JX

**OVER £10,000 IN POETRY PRIZES
TO BE WON!**

Send an SAE for details on our New Year 2003 competition!